Night's Body

Night's Body

Poems by George Keithley

Turning Point

Published by Turning Point
P.O. Box 541106
Cincinnati, OH 45254-1106

ISBN: 9781936370290
LCCN: 2011923034

Poetry Editor: Kevin Walzer
Business Editor: Lori Jareo

Visit us on the web at www.turningpointbooks.com

Also by George Keithley

Poetry

The Starry Messenger
The Midnight Train
Living Again
Earth's Eye
The Burning Bear
To Bring Spring
Scenes from Childhood
Song in a Strange Land
The Donner Party

Fiction

Ring of Fire
Flesh and Dust

Drama

The Best Blood of the Country

Literary Journalism

Themes in American Literature, Co-Editor

Acknowledgments

I wish to acknowledge, with thanks, the editors of the following publications, in which these poems have appeared: *Agni*, "The Sea"; *Alaska Quarterly Review*, "The Driver"; *The Amicus Journal*, "First Morning" and "When They Leave"; *Ararat*, "Tree House"; *Barnabe Mountain Review*, "Living Again"; *The Bridge, 7*, "Wild Horse Sanctuary"; *Colorado Review*, "Black Water"; *Columbia*, "Dusk" and "Hawks"; *Elkhorn Review*, "Raccoons"; *5AM*, "Among the Leaves", "Homage to Akhmatova", "Painted Horses", and "Summer Night"; *The Kenyon Review*, "Chiaroscuro"; *The Kerf*, "Autumn" and "Enjoy the Land"; *Literary Imagination*, "The Half-Dark"; *Manoa*, "Joy" and "Old Holy Men"; *Poetry Now*, "Looking at the Man"; *The Sewanee Review*, "The Dance", "Eleven Sketches in Charcoal", "The Mare", "Meditation at Mill Creek", "Nighthawk", "The Rice Grower's Daughter", and "Trio"; *Studia Mystica*, "Now" and "Warm Rain"; *Uzzano*, "Fishing the Sky" and "Old Women Wading in the Sea"; *Volt*, "Memory" and "The Pond"; *Wild Duck Review*, "The Deer Come Down", "The Storm Cellar" and "Winter Night"; *Wild Earth*, "The Kill"; and *Windhover*, "Doctor Paracelsus".

For several lines of poetry by Anna Akhmatova and one line by Osip Mandelstam, I'm indebted to the lucid translations by Judith Hemschemeyer, *The Complete Poems of Anna Akhmatova*, Zephyr Press; Lyn Coffin, *Anna Akhmatova: Poems*, W.W. Norton; and Roberta Reeder, *Anna Akhmatova, Poet and Prophet*, St. Martin's Press.

"When They Leave" received the Pushcart Prize and has been reprinted in *Pushcart Prize XVI;*

also in *Poetry from the Amicus Journal* and *Organic Advocate*. "Raccoons" and "Tree House" appear in the Heatherstone Press *Anniversary Edition* anthology; "Tree House" also appears in *What's Become of Eden*, Slapering Hol Press. "Dusk" is reprinted in *This Little Bit of Earth*, Valley Oaks Press, and "Autumn" in the Heyday Books anthology *Highway 99: A Literary Journey*. "The Sea" and "Winter Night" were reprinted in *Wild Duck Review*, and "Winter Night" appears in *River Voices* anthology, PWJ Publishing. "First Morning" has appeared in *Wild Duck Review* (reprinted), on the website *e-Amicus*, and in the anthology *Poetry Comes Up Where It Can*, The University of Utah Press. "Meditation at Mill Creek" appears in the *International Poetry Calendar*, Alhambra Publishing (Belgium).

Thanks also to the New England Poetry Club for the Gretchen Warren Award for "Joy" and the Daniel Varoujan Award for "Tree House."

Special thanks to my wife Carol. To Liz and Kathy. To Clare, Steve, and Tristan. To Chris, Fiona, and Ian. To Lydia and Duncan and in memory to Charlotte. To Kathleen McPartland, and to Joanne Allred for her invaluable assistance. And to Joe Brendle, Clark Brown, Ray Hurt, and Lou Nevins. All have helped more than I can say.

For

Dennis and Loretta Schmitz

and for

Gary and Linda Thompson

Contents

I

At Four in the Morning

Caught in the crossfire of artillery, the peasants had
evacuated this valley. . .Only their dogs remained,
ghostly creatures that hunted their pitiful prey by day
and howled in the night. At four in the morning,
when the moon rose white as a picked bone, the
whole village bayed at the dead divinity.
Antoine de Saint-Exupery

Down there, the young bulls sleep behind the single
strand of their electric fence. It is four o'clock in the
morning.
Thomas Merton

Painted Horses

Horses after first light browsed the border
of the plateau. The sun had burned away
a thin mist; earth gleamed. Birds circled, screeching.

Because of their wild grace how huge the horses
loomed in our eyes. How stern when they stalked us
through a fitful sleep. Finding them larger than life,

on cavern walls—temples of the imagination—
we painted them in proportion to their spirit:
Running wild, they'd nip or bite each other—

Sometimes in pleasure but often with malice.
They ran the way a full river flows, headlong,
assuming the shape of the land then swiftly

overwhelming it. Round-eyed, whinnying.
The fierce ones charging, blowing and frothing.
Fights were brief but furious. Kicking, chomping.

Or they reared, snorting, and pummeled with their hooves.
Today we excavate the battered bones;
the scarred hides are preserved in mudbanks, tar.

What do we know that is sacred? Water,
rocks. Without these the weather of each day
is insignificant, crags cast deep shadows

then withdraw them, they offer no shelter
to a troubled creature. Fire—we carried it
flickering from the mouths of caves. Down dark

hillsides, the steep terrain broken, footing
uncertain. Cautiously we crossed creeks; never
more than one torch upon the water. Or

more frequently followed the tumbling, coursing
water through gullies illuminated
only by wings of flame. Which we brought on,

wavering, flaring, into sunlit fields. Fowl
fled through the brush or flapped above it, striving,
desperate. Birds bewildered us. Their cries were ours,

but their flight, their songs, suggested another world.
Taking on their plumage and their piercing eyes,
the distant heavens settled among the trees.

Trees were worshiped, dreaded. What other life
joined beauty and necessity? Grass. Windswept swales
where the nimble-footed horses romped or grazed;

where mares cajoled their spindly foals to stand
tottering. Testing balance, vision, and nerve.
Learning attention. Alert then to the scent of smoke

thickening the air, throbbing under its dark warning,
all turned with one mind and raced across the green plateau
thirty thousand years before this morning.

Joy

The storm blunders through the street, flapping
every awning. A downpour drenches
shoppers caught on the walks, the clerk
on her hurried errand, whipping her skirt
against her legs. Together we reach
the aged bandstand, shingles gone
from a gaping roof, the only shelter
in the green plaza. One summer night
Sidney Bechet played here,
his clarinet singing that sad joy
that was his voice. Is it the wind
or rain that makes you laugh? We lean
close. Your hand in my coat. What
a storm! Black elms blaze! The wind roars
on, roars on, tossing branches. Rain
batters the empty benches.
                              Step back,
look. Water from the splayed roof spills
splat splat around our feet.
Yes, and your hair! How it shines!
How happy I am you're here! But this rain!
It's so loud we turn to watch the wind
buffet the roses, the hyacinths. Now
it plunges down the footpath, shaking
all the shrubbery, bright as silver.
It takes hold of the blue phonebooth
by the flowerbed—a wobbly glass
door swings open, claps shut. Rain swamps

the blossoms. We love each other, we can't
speak. I hold you and we shiver like the grass.

Living Again

Then he remembered the blue house where they'd lived.
Her hair nesting on her shoulder as in this photo.
The firm weight of her breast. His hand opened.
The frame struck the floor; glass shattered—

He tore his shirt to reach the pain. Now
he choked on the silence in the cabin.
No breath. The door banged open. He stumbled

through the pines. Into the meadow. Pools of snow-
melt among the budding thistles, lupine.
Still he did not cry out. His mouth a mute O.

Above the silver river he saw a hawk flicker.
His chest on fire, he forgot his right hand
full of excuses. Fell among mule-ear. Grass

growing dim. Waking, on his hands and knees,
he noticed the pain that gripped his heart
had eased into his shoulders. Deep

in his belly his breath welled up. Again
the hawk flashed its blood-red tail
in the wind. He rose, slowly. Saw tawny

cattails nodding. Poppies. The first purple
thistles. He listened. For what? When
he was about to die he'd remembered the dark

rain in her voice. Spring rain falling all night
in the Sierra, lifting the river above its bank,
drenching the green meadow, waking sun-gold blossoms.

Then did his heart recover its rhythm, his mind
its balance? He took two steps. Heard water churn;
slosh sedge grass, slap rocks. A chill light

rushed downstream. When he saw it shiver past
the black mudbank already he'd begun to choose
this life in which our words follow one another
to the end: snowmelt, granite, hawk, poppies, river.

Warm Rain

Night and day the rain spills its silence
over us. South of Galilee not one hand
tends the orchards; the pipe-fed fields
idle on the floor of the Ghor
or *Al Ghawr,* absorb the dripping stillness.
Twelve days' rain drenches the valley.
High water in the wadis. Only
these girls wrapped in grey wool
each morning gather by the river.

Brooding sky. Gravel soil
swept away, water
roiling downstream,
splashing into the salt
slow sea. Green reeds
glowing. Two girls lean over

the bank. Laughing, they lower
their bare feet into the flow.

Together they unbundle
rolls of soiled clothes
to catch the current
flapping past. Upriver
the sky flashes silver—
A stand of slender young
willows washing
their hair in the high wind.

Under the rain the river
Jordan rises, trembling,
the lean brown arm
of the dead
god growing restless in the reeds.

Hawks

1

Late March—late in the afternoon the first hawks
return. Gliding across the cornfield, they veer
above the barn where the mice wintered. Drift
downriver to the marsh. Discover the deep basket
tight-woven in the reeds, a blackbird's nest.
The toad's trill halts. Swooping into the trees,
complaining, hawks catch the gleaming light—
Among maples, elms, a ruddy plumage we'd
half-forgotten. Their fierce faces open:
How could it be spring without that wild cry,
kee-ear, kee-year! A muskrat flattens, blackens,
slithering under the iridescent water—

2

> Twilight. Small wind. How
> the river glimmers!
>
> The red-shouldered hawk
> circles the marsh. On
> still wings it descends
> into dusk. At night
> roosts under the sad
> eyes of Orion
> who hunts for us all,
> his dog at his heel;
> shy Andromeda
> chained to the onyx
> sky. Again the stars

wheel their tales across
the listening dark
like prayers the tongue turns
over, turns over,
the cycle never
ending in this world
or in the other—
Black Elk told us, "Birds
build their nests in circles
for their religion
is the same as ours."

Asleep, the hawk hides
one eye under its wing.

3
Dawn. Cold mist clings to the rushes. It lifts
with the sun, the sky deepens. Hawks
flex their wings, thrash the air, climb thermals—
Soar above the river, the pasture. Under the sun
the shadows of their wings are dark knives—
The chipmunk squeals in the busy grass. Swerving
across the shallows, a hawk plummets. Plucks
the muskrat, web-toed, fumbling toward its den—

They settle, fretting their wings, in limbs over
the water's edge. Midday. The hawks perch
among the elms, their stark voices rising
and falling in the green memory of the marsh.

The Driver

After I'd steered the ambulance off the road
I coaxed it across an open pasture,
rocking to a halt in fresh April mud
while overhead the rack of warning-lights
whirled its circus colors. First I shut down
our shrill siren. Then blacked the lights. Once
their dazzle thrilled me—now it chills my blood.
At four in the morning the full moon flooded
Butte Creek Canyon with a cold white glow
that marbled the water in light and shadow.

Before us Search and Rescue had planted flares.
Unsteady stars, they flamed up, hissed, flickered
over the slick creekside, revealing tape
that sealed the 'dicovery site'—bold yellow
like the body bag laid out upon the bank.
Nearby we found the subject's pocketwatch.
Twin shell casings. His trail map soaked to pulp.
Two gin bottles. Binoculars. One lens,
already shattered, popped at my thumb's touch.
Detritus of the self—a man I almost knew.

Off duty we'd played interminable chess,
a pair of bunglers. Fondly, he thought he lived
for his family; his work. To a wilderness
firefighter the hours had seemed infinite,
watching the wind chafe the meadow. Returning
to find his wife loading the stationwagon,
taking their children to live with her lover.

Clearly suicide. Still the sheriff impounded
his gun. One deputy shot photos. My young
paramedics finished probing; signed papers.

They hoisted the stretcher on board with a care
beyond their years, the yellow bag turning
orange beneath our emergency lamp. Shifting
the corpse to the fixed cot, their work was done.
I latched both doors. Briefly the engine stalled.
Then, throbbing, it lifted us free of the field
and—headlights only—we eased onto the road.
No wailing siren. No revolving lights
to speed us through traffic. It was not yet dawn
and the dead have all the time in the world.

When They Leave

When they leave the world will be at peace
forever. A room with wide windows
shut against the weather. Wind
beyond the glass bending the brilliant maples.
Will we hear wings beating out of those trees?

Who can inhabit the unholy sleep
of the soul once they wander
silently away? Who'll bark, howl,
bray, croak, whirr, whinny, all
together raise their joyful noise? None

of these creatures who breed and birth
their young and feed
so near to us
a man forgets
the grace granted to each one—

Cattle
because they are convenient—

Coyotes
because they are not—

The cats
which remind us of our debts—

The sentimental dog who swallows his pride
and happily prevails

by licking plates.

Ordinary horses
who carry their ancient hearts under ours.

Also the bristling hog we hate and eat.

The customary spotted goat we know
will never acknowledge its guilt—

Black clouds of crows who strut
among the muddy furrows
at seedtime. Hosts of locusts
floating like smoke over the fields—
The brown bats in love with our streetlamps.

Droves of animals who mate and thrive
and swarm before our eyes only
to disappear when we dream
because they are too innocent
to survive.

Autumn

Autumn, old mother, you bless with lightning bolts.
Thunder shudders caprock, rolls down the canyon.
Storm clouds break above the foothills, swelling
Horseshoe Lake, flooding Butte Creek—
Out of Mad Woman Meadow a sleek dog trots home,
burrs knotted in its long ears, its switching tail.

In town the streets run red with rain,
pistachios bleed under our feet.
Persimmon trees, wind-plundered, clutch their bare fruit.
Irascible oaks shake dark fists. What's this
silver light? It glosses chiseled grey
tombstones tucked behind an iron fence—

The rusted red truck swerves to avoid
the dog struck dead in the road
beside the cemetery. Ducking into the rain,
a man and woman leave their pickup, lift the lean dog
into the bed and drape a painter's tarp over it.
They drive down the spattered road without a word.

Mother of rain, grass, dusk. You teach us
the end of life. Now at the last
daylight hour the storm surges, dies out. Gone
is the green scent of hay drifting across the highway.
Beanfields, sodden, blue-black, glimmer like the sky.
Under ghostly sycamores the creek rolls, tumbles

down its rockbed: the voice of my father before his stroke,
his merriment irrepressible as water. Do trees listen
to our words as we attend to their thrumming music?
I want them to hear the spring concert solo
Jean played, her shy eyes proud of the blue
tunic and gold braid of the school band.

The clarinet coal-black in her pale hands. Head bowed
to applause. Her bell of brown hair by summer's end
lost to leukemia. Two months after the funeral
her sister caught by the midnight train
far from town, her boyfriend's car
stalled on the crossing above our flooded fields.

Mother of all that I remember—
Your rains wash my eyes,
I see the blue earth breathing low and still.
In this soil you gather my family,
my friends. They wait for me
as the wind waits and the waters settle.

After the flashing storm, under the turning maples,
in your streams the light's blood spills, gleams.
In you I learn the rhythm that rises
and falls in my heart. Here
in the deep fields, in crimson water—
In the slow sacred blood of our mother.

II

Winter Nocturnes

What's this? Darkness in town?
It could be!
Tonight comes winter's first
Hard freeze. Settle down.
Anna Akhmatova

First Morning

Autumn is finished—yesterday a flash
storm, the worst since my father's death,
then last night's freeze. At once granite
outcrop wears a milky glaze. All
the lean hemlocks are sheathed in ice.
At dawn walking from the meadow
to the woods I wish for the warmth
of his voice. A peaceable man—only
injustice angered him. How might
we meet again if not hiking
in these frosted fields? No hunter,
he loved to discover animals
in their habitat then leave them
undisturbed. Which he thought just.
"They earn their peace among us.
Let them be." The wren in her nest.
The half-dozen frogs surviving
—who can say how—in a bog-hole.
Two owls attracted to the gloom
of the horse barn.
                        His patience will take
years to learn—it's time I start home
to my own children. Emerging
from a stand of pines shagged with cold,
the needles silvered overnight,
I surprise a fox and he bolts
to safety. An old-timer. His
brushy tail barely twitches
the white grass and leaves little

trace. Drops of ice sparkle among
manzanita. Where my path ends
in light an opaque blue sheen clings
to the county road. It's the first
morning of winter and the world
is made of glass the heart must break.

Trio

1

When Clara wrote that her husband had attempted suicide
(Schumann in robe and slippers bolted the house—
hurled himself into the frigid Rhine)
Brahms came at once to Bonn. He was twenty-one.
Could he be mistaken? He feared for Robert,
while Clara, mother of seven, quivered like a bride.
He was undone by his desire. And her distress.

He wanted to hold her to his breast,
knowing the embrace meant more than comfort.

2

Might he bow his boyish head before her grief
and kiss her hands? They were not delicate,
though she appeared to be. Agile, yet tender;
hands capable of toil or exquisite performance.

He murmured his farewell and fled for home.
It was early March—the night bright and cold.
Work alone might release him from his shame;
weren't these two—man and wife—his dearest friends?

3

In his study he drew the tattered drapes.
On the floor the pile of familiar manuscripts;
a glass, a solitary saucer. The room
of a single-minded man. His cigars,
twin candelabra, two music stands. Striving

to complete his Piano Trio in B,
he labored all night though the fire was down.

He sat then, silent. In the diminishing dark
he wished again to kiss her trembling hands.

The Kill

For three days the pack had trailed the great elk
herd through thin forest of pine and maple,
the wolves lean and limber in the mottled light
falling on their fur. Sunlight silvered it
but in the shade they were grey or grey-black,
and their trot was so effortless they seemed
to be dreaming. On the fourth morning the herd
fled into a meadow where the wolves attacked
an aging buck, snapping at his flanks and rump.
Once they'd dropped him they tore into his hide.

Their teeth ripped the buck open. Their breathing
grew labored; rasping, narrow chests heaving—
Long snouts dripping as they glutted on venison.

Feeding until dusk, they shared the carcass
with cawing ravens wafting up and down,
plucking bits of flesh then prancing away.

When they'd eaten all but the long shards of bone,
antlers, hooves, portions of the shredded hide,
the wolves cleansed themselves of the elk's dense scent.

They lapped at their fur, ruffled and bloodied.
They swabbed it with slobber then matted it
with their mouths, meticulously tonguing it.

Those that paired off went on bathing. Rising
through their fatigue they turned to lick the ears

or spine of a partner, another. Soon
their coats glowed like woodsmoke in the moonlight.
Retreating among the trees, the pack gathered
itself in a clearing. Trampling their tight
circle into the grass, the wolves lay down
in the peace of all that lives, all that dies,
all that's holy here. Then they shut their eyes
and slept with their hearts beating beneath the night.

The Half-Dark

At dusk when the wind falls the first thick flurries
brighten the air but it soon darkens.
The ticking sound of the snow
is the sound of time settling
on the tin roof of the newsstand
(its faulty lamp flickering on and off)
and over the traffic slowing, almost halting, in the street.

While the city sleeps it remembers snow
piled streetside in dusky banks. A wreath
of moonlight—the ice encrusted fountain.
The innumerable angles of legs tucked
behind each desk or climbing stairs
in the half-dark of the soul. Now
it dreams the blue buildings of our breath.

Crossing Spirit Lake in Early Winter

Eyes burning. The slashing snow.
Since dusk a gale had swept
the frozen lake—snow drifted
underfoot—our boots slipped.
Night left but the thin light
of glazed ice or none at all.
"Stay close!" we warned. Most gripped
hands. Or linked arms. Only
our boldest—those few—broke
free. While they fled across
new ice we heard that first
crack! Another. The third
like a distant lightning
strike. But no more. How far
had they gone? When the wind-
blown snow settled we found
no trace. Then all the living
witnessed an apparition:

Every face luminous
with its fever—the brief
haste of a flare until
it faded before us. Yes,
and the pulse in each voice—
how their souls urged us not
to lose heart. As we pushed
on we cried out their names
over the snow-scrim and bare
ice. No distinct trail to track.

Finally, "Are you there?"
we pleaded. Searching, slow
step by step through the dark.

Wild Horse Sanctuary

1
Joan Burda's truck bounces down the road through thin-falling
  snow,
almost sleet. At the run-in shed she racks half the hay,
spreading the remainder among clumps of winter grass
so the herd can feed freely. This morning the black
stallion has led them down to Lost Child Creek—
Two hundred ponies roam the range to forage in the fine snow.
Three shelter in a stand of cottonwoods then straggle over.
The snowfall, no longer slanting, thickens
as Joan skims the trough
and the mare approaches:

Ears forward.
Eyes warm, curious.
A red roan with scars that ridge her cheek.
Scars mark her neck. Her flank and thigh. "Hello—"

2
Though the mustangs heed no names Joan calls her *Lady*.
This roan who hid from her husband Ben (ranching
twelve years in Alberta to protest the war).
Fled from the volunteers on prison furlough
mucking a run-in, mending fence, weeding.
Fled them to foal among the alders gleaming
with that tender spring green that stops your heart
down in Crow Canyon where she dropped her colt.
The second night a cougar tore into it. Now
she shies from the creek, awaits the steaming truck.

That other pair amble up.
"Leave a bite for Lady—"
Spotty colts
they spurn the hay.
Won't touch her
tank-water either,
loping out to join the herd.

3
Hammering with their hooves, they crack the ice in the creek,
then lower their muzzles to drink. Her gaze trails them—
the colts kicking up new snow, nipping one another—
down the distant meadow broken by drifts, scrub grass.
Stippled with pine, aspen; the boughs barely white.
Joan Burda blinks back the cold.
Tells herself what matters is not gratitude:
She doesn't wish to tame them.
To nurture them.
To break down

their bred-in-the-blood habits. Only
to save what is wild in the heart
and mind and leave it
an open range—all this room—to run.

Old Holy Men

Tonight a sudden snowfall chills the plaza,
one corner trimmed with Christmas lights—
Bulbs blink in the bushes, the lamp-lit snow
glitters in a crèche of papier mâché.
Snow nestles in the bare elms. Beyond,
migrant families climb for cover
onto the warped bandstand.
                              Four men
unwrap bedrolls, two nuns in black
distribute blankets among the young
couples: Chicano, Maidu, white mothers
hurry their children to the open pavilion.

One boy and one thin girl hold back.
They bolt into the dark. Hurl
snowballs, dodge behind white benches.
Under the elms they laugh and fall,
wrestling in the fresh snow.
                              Together
they skid down the slick path to find
Joseph, a father, life-size, frayed robe
across his shoulder. Mary is pale
in her prim cowl; her infant all
bathed in light in the bulb-strung stable.
A shelter without walls, water, heat.

Breathless and flushed they stand, rapt,
beneath the trees. Her hand in his.
Why do they look from the tethered mule

to the straw floor where two parents kneel
over their only hope?
                    The slim girl,
the boy, restless, turn to each other—
In the gaudy cold they glow
like old holy men who discover
the shrine they sought, immortal
image of desire, is no more
than the mirror of their own bold thought.

Eleven Sketches in Charcoal

French trapper's drawings abandoned in an
Oglala camp on the Powder River,
Wyoming Territory, Winter 1866

1

The four who stole the soldiers' horses drive them
into the wind without rest. Dawn to dusk.
A wolf wind, swift and sharp, biting their faces.
They ride without reins or bits or halters.

From the fort on the plateau clear to the river
swales of old snow glimmer
between patches of prairie grass speckled
and pale as a spring fawn.

2

> When the riders cross the river
> into camp the ice under-
> foot (black, opaque)
> never quakes. It
> rings hard as iron.

3

Their wives, turning four ways, chant their names
over blankets, knives, a bone-handled hatchet.
A bonfire blazes—

(The geometric beadwork of their dresses.)

4

The trader's coffee and heavy kettles.
His free-hand map of the river
to this point. Unadorned
the rawhide bag that preserves his sketches.

5

Dogs slather a girl's hand for scraps.

6

> In the lodge hides hang
> beside ornamental skulls,
> distended claws, strips
> of dried meat. Quivers
> bristling arrows. Below
> on the beaten floor
> spears, stone clubs.
> The haft of an axe.

7

> Swathed in a remnant of
> buffalo robe a stack
> of no more than four
> single-shot rifles.

> To one side the word
> *effroi* appears:
> Fright? Or dread?

8

Children chase their voices through the cottonwoods.
What calls them back?

Flutes. Whistles. Pulsing drums.
All night dancers, shuffling, circle the flames.

9
Couples, seated, wrap themselves in shadows.
Darting among the dancers
with her armful of broken boughs
grandmother feeds the fire—
Sparks leap and laugh. A bright cold night.

10
      Warriors enter the ring—a few
      rapid strokes. Markings
      imprecise. For the hour
      thickens now with smoke
      as the throng whirls and
      the hand surrenders its will
      in one irregular scrawl:
      Je suis pris de terreur.

11
No signature but beside this final scene
effroi is repeated.
In haste—smeared.

Thin indolent cattle crowd
close for warmth. Mules
edge among them. Left
alone the horses steam in the dark.

Winter Night

Moonlight—fresh snow fills the meadow—
the blizzard that buried the road
beyond the storm-fence has blown off.
No wind lifting skittish clouds of
powder. No tracks but ours. Only
the owl's shadow gliding over
Alder Creek. Through the trees we see
the work winter does, the snowfield
glittering, widening, using
up all the spare white light the way
a river stretches in the sun . . .
Suddenly the sheen of this ice-
sharp wind that brings tears to your eyes.
Our voices, while we hike downhill,
construct a life more plausible
than the words that glow before us,
then dissolve in the dark.
                              Until
we find the young fox the owl gorged
itself on. Blood and bone. Kneeling,
we cover it with shallow snow
dogs will dig tomorrow.
                              Silence
thrives in the black night and we know
at the heart of this clarity
is sorrow. This is what I want
to understand as we turn home
beneath the stars, their fervent fire:
How solitude survives us. When

I reach for your hand you offer
it and we touch without speech, we
embrace. Then stand here together
in this moment, this white meadow,
which takes our breath away and fills
us with wonder. The cold world so
still its beauty shines regardless
of the cub's blood, the drifted road.

III

Women at Night

"Do you feel it, too?" said Linda, as she spoke to her mother
with the special voice that women use at night to each other
as though they spoke in their sleep or from some hollow
cave—"Don't you feel that it is coming towards us?"
Katherine Mansfield

It was full moon while I was down at Takaunga, and
the beauty of the radiant, still nights was so perfect
that the heart bent under it. You slept with the doors
open to the silver Sea . . . One night a row of Arab
dhows came along, close to the coast, running
noiselessly before the monsoon, a file of brown
shadow-sails under the moon.
Isak Dinesen

Chiaroscuro

In autumn when seagulls went winging over the Seine
and the implacable plane trees were turning yellow
she chose to sketch them in charcoal. Under shivering
chestnut trees on the Champs-Élysées she studied
three leaves spattered on the pavement. Pausing
on her familiar route to the Rodin museum,
beside a brick wall she bent to photograph
the spikey fruit fallen onto the damp stones
at her feet. For a later day. Rising, she saw
drizzle gleaming on mansard rooftops, a host
of swallows flocking home. The weather turned her
toward her upstairs flat overlooking the Metro
and the market where she bought her tin of tea.

Also, for her stewpot, the blushing pink pig's
head collared with a wreath of flowers. Pointedly
she set down her sketchpad and raised a window
to await the evening. Long ago she'd learned
how a line in darkness differs from a line in light:

How each form acquires its depth with a certain
loss of identity. As dusk arrives freighted
with threats and promises, rumbling through the city.

A train besmirched by smoke, steam. Doors clatter
open, passengers abandon the day's journey,
crowding the platform. No longer would she draw
trains leaving behind their twin silver tracks
in echoes of light and shadow, knowing the more

a line repeats itself the less it grows.

While she watched a young woman struggle
to unfurl her umbrella streetlights sputtered on.

Beneath the staircase to the elevated train
a man in a coal-dark vest sat strumming
Granada. Then Villa-Lobos. Sor. Debussy.
Standing before her window drinking black
tea laced with honey, she asked herself
if what we wish is the soul of what we are—
Now she was neither working nor finished working
she became, as she wished, one with the shadows,
listening to the sonorous rain of the guitar.

The Sea

> It is a human sharing in the rhythm of the sea
> and the moon
> and animal breeding
> and the stars.
>
> Ernesto Cardenal, *Love*

Helpless her hands lose hold, slip away.
As though night hides an undertow
which lifts her warm weight on its arm.
Along the dark she drifts
out of sight—
A solid sea-wall divides the surf
from the shore splashed with rocks.

When the man wades out to find her
the moon pulls up its anchor.
It slides free of the tide—
The hull of his soul sails on
the sky, his body is a buoy
in the black seams of the waves.
A drunken crew dances on the deck.

In sleep we float far apart. Voyage
in different dreams that wreck
in the wind. And fear
death in the deep bed. Then swim
toward land. Birdsong. The blue scent
of wild lilac. Suddenly here we stand
on the stones of consciousness, shining, short of breath—

Dusk

The path below the cabin breaks through brush, rubble.

Across the clearing ponderosa and lodgepole pine
(twilight is caught in the crowns of the trees)
as we start downhill to the lake. You dreamed
last night of another girl growing up
in Nevada. It was her turn to prop bottles
along the low fence. Unflinching, you braced
the rifle against your shoulder. Sighted.
Fired—glass exploding! Shards sparkling!
Delight dancing in your blue eyes. Hiking
through the leaning shadows I think of the boy
I shagged flies for; then jogged across the field
to take my swings. Every warm evening
until that summer night his brother Jack,
racing his black bike on the new highway
out of town, sped into twilight, the swift
onrushing truck.
        At the 4th of July picnic
we played Capture-the-Flag. Jeannie dodging
fireflies. Was she eleven? Her thin voice
rising: "I can run! I'm in remission."

How many more, remembered, mute? Children
forever in your memory or mine. No
loss that can't be lost again if we whisper
their names. Where the path narrows red needles
yield that resin scent. We pause stock-still.
Then slip out to the shore together and alone.

Where did they go? The others? Wings muffled,
a horned owl glides over. Searching, searching.
Dusk lifts the last light from the pines,
the night wind ripples the water. Listen—
All the souls in the lake are eager to speak.

Homage to Anna Akhmatova

1

We have murdered time but it will rise
in judgment of our acts, she believes;
this is our hope and our fate. Yes,
this is the resurrection we await—
Her first husband had been arrested
by Lenin's *Cheka*. Without trial
he was stood against a wall and shot.
Buried with countless others in a pit.
Now, though their son Lev is innocent
of any crime, for eighteen years
he's held in prison to silence her.
Interrogated, beaten, isolated,
sentenced to hard labor. Finally
condemned to die like his father
should she *fail to cooperate
with the state* . . . In the prison yard
every morning a firing squad
assembles. Rope, sidearms, rifles.

2

Immediately after Stalin orders
her books confiscated, destroyed,
a dozen solitary men and women
recite her lines to preserve them,
invisible. Hurriedly she gathers
her papers (notebooks, diary, letters);
all that haven't been seized she burns
in her flat.
           Night and day fearing

for another's life—it's her son's;
it might be yours or anyone's—
Anna is compliant. Or she
appears to be. As with her slow
long-legged stride she navigates
the gloom of a northern night, smoke
driven to ground by the drenching
rain. No light at the corner. She
gropes for the stairs. A doorlatch slips.

3
Tall and gaunt, she stoops to enter.
The tassled lamp reveals her eyes,
pale, austere; its shadows sharpen
her angular Old Believer's face.
Lord, this sudden fire! Her heart.
One moment for the pain to lapse.
Composed now. A quiet greeting.
The brief embrace before her host
offers a taste of pastry. Tea. Then
with a quavering in her throat
she delivers from memory
her guest's unforgiving poetry
as clear as water and as necessary:

"I, half-mad, mourning the past . . .
the black whisper of misfortune . . .
I am forbidden to appear anywhere."

Anna, her head tilted back, listens
to the fearful tremolo in her friend's
voice: "Blood smells only like blood . . .

And if they gag my exhausted mouth . . .
time will rise like a corpse."
                              In return
she, in a low melodious tone,
recites her beloved Pushkin. Blok.
Tsvetayeva—dazzling, distraught—
and Osip Mandelstam: "Ten steps
away no one hears our speeches."
This, Anna prays, is true. Rising
to leave, she retrieves her shawl.

4
Just shy of the doorstep she searches
the sulphurous murk, discerning
that pair near the stairwell. What
then has changed? Nothing! Wet, chilled,
the two agents stalking her lurk
beneath a neighbor's windowshade,
drinking under broad umbrellas,
stamping their boots for warmth. So,
Lev lives still! Still the terror. Each
night they shadow her with such disdain
they dare her to discover them. While
in her soul reverberates the threat
she knows by heart: *Should you persist
in writing poems, or publish . . . If
you protest his sentence; confer
with foreign authors or complain
to treacherous reporters . . .* Will
they trail her home? No sign of her
alarm. With that deliberate
dignity of one who fears your pain

and imminent death more than her own,
she descends the stairs. At her feet
the dark street shivers in the rain.

The Rice Grower's Daughter

Stepping out from the orchard on a summer evening
a woman sees her father's rice fields burning.
And witnesses, too, the terror of the wrens.

Hundreds of small brown birds, sedge wrens,
frantically climbing into the black air.

Beating the air, they flap like bits of rags
torn from one another and flung there
above the blaze. Now, as the flame leaps,

they veer silently down through the smoke
where the only voice is the rush of the fire—

A shrill cry that flies upward and never stops.

She longs to call out. To warn them away:
Go on—! Whatever you do! But she can't
wake herself to speak because she knows
she has not dreamed this. Who would want to?

Old Women Wading in the Sea

Seven women working past twilight
          stoop to gather
      the spilling sea. They rise,
   laugh: *O-hoo-ah!* Violet waves
       swell, subside. *Ai!* Sand fails
         to support
      their fetching feet. They cry,

Ai! They are *yee!* Afraid of falling!
        Laden with luck
      they trudge onto the beach,
    streams of pearl pouring down their breasts
     to pool at their heels. While
       the full moon
     flowers, they wring their skirts.

At dusk we purchase—*Deux, oui*—conch shells
       and your coral
     necklace from the ancient
   women wading hip-deep beyond
     the shore. Their skirts—amber,
      lime—drenched in
    warm surf where bone fish swim.

Hands so frail they tremble offering
      treasure: florid
     shells, fluted beads. The price
   a whisper. *Bon. Merci.* As they
     turn away we notice

their hair is
actually silver

wound in buns behind their heads.

The Pond

1
"You tell me," he said. "A dream, a lie, a story?"
Did I think the soul is anything at all, he asked,
and his voice, always faint, quavered in the mild air.

After a spring shower sunlight sponging the sidewalk dry.

"I know it's not flesh and blood," he said. "But whose dream?
Whose story?" A troubled priest, he no longer drinks
but he still shakes. Too jittery to offer the eucharist,
the trembling host. How could I not know his shame?
"I've become the thing I dreaded being. This empty
black suit. Threadbare. A sight to scare children."

We walked beside a steaming street. Cars blaring.

2
Amid couples clasping hands the bitter but welcome
aroma of coffee had lifted the city to its feet—
Window-shoppers; their glassy faces. The stained beard
murmuring into its newspaper. The cluster of men
and women straining to read a marquee. Necks craned
like ducks worried by changeable weather. Quiet eyes
heavenward. Why then did I remember a small pond?
Almost winter in the woods. Cold, damp. Dense clouds
low and darkening. Weighted with what? Rain or snow.
Impossible to tell beforehand although you see
its imminence in the level water: the certain
coming of it. In time how it disturbs the pond.

Even the deep woods. "Is it, then, the fever
of every changing hour?" he asked: "Is it how
we know the loss that flies from us forever?"

3
Ahead of us, two women, buoyant in April dresses,
hurried, heels clicking. Stopping for the corner light.

"I didn't see you last night at the party."
"Sorry I missed it. But *you* said you'd call."
"I couldn't speak. To anyone."
"Was Alice——?"
 "I found her naked in our bedroom."
"Again? The slut."
"Asleep on the rug."
"How do you stand it? If my——"
 "I don't know where he was. Or care."
"But *you* had to wake her."
"I dragged her across the floor by her hair."

They walked on.

4
"I have to believe the soul is more than anger and pain,"
he pleaded as we crossed the street.
Hurrying belatedly the way men run
who are nearly too old to run, dragging our shadows.

"How do we know?"

"Don't be a damned fool. You're my friend."
His voice trembled: "Trust me."

Rain or snow.

The Dance

While lanterns lolled above the sweet spring grass
fresh-mowed for the party—gleams of light
lilting like a dance of bees among the boughs—
we lay in the orchard. And drank little wine
because the fragrance of your auburn hair
was all I knew of longing. I spoke your name
with the darkness in my throat and you whispered
mine more clearly than I'd ever heard it
uttered. Or hoped to. The delicate tongues
of leaves in the mouth of the sky. The night
wind warm, yes, and your skirt fell from your knees.
But voices climbed the hill. Your father called
a reel. Two fiddles sang while couples clapped.

Memory spares us nothing touched by love—
You wept without a sound while my fingers brushed
your blouse—apple blossoms—then we walked down
among the last trees, their shifting shadows,
into the light to join the others. Pairs
twirling, taking hold, in time releasing.
Women whirling their wide skirts over
all the lawn. Men young and old unwilling
to shed their fine coats, sweating with pleasure.
Yet they stopped to stare at your tears. Tell me
tonight what's more dear than your hand in mine
and that proud toss of your hair? All these years.

IV

In the Night of Unknowing

God is nearer in the night.
                    Adam Ilius, a Niger
                    child on his first
                    caravan in the Sahara

The Deer Come Down

1

It is summer. Our sixth year of drought. The deer come down
from the parched mountain meadow pale as a hayfield,
the mule-ear cropped, manzanita plucked bare,
lupine wilting in an empty wind.

The last snow gleams on a granite slope where the sun flashes.

A fallen pine shredded by beetles disgorges its red scent.
Out of habit the herd tries the spring rainpool—
It is baked, chalky, the fringe of sawgrass rasping.
After they forage on pennyroyal
like our souls they come down from the dry heights
seeking water. They risk free-fall
on that steep grade to follow their thirst
through a stand of brittle pines.
Eyes dark and clear
with one desire.
Is this all? Or
what dread wisdom guides them
so far downstream
outflanking the fishing camp,
the silted well,
the emigrant girl's gravestone furred by moss?

Heedless of human intention—they have never known
regret—the deer ignore the dog yawping,
straining its chain. The gun
gleaming in the corner of the poacher's cabin.

2

You signal silence, your finger touches your lips—
A doe halts in the dusty clearing. Spindly,
delicate, she dares us to approach.
Moist eyes search the mottled woods.

Finding two truant fawns, she turns, trots off.
They amble after her. While we watch the herd
emerge from the shadows of the trees
the sun pours down on Mill Creek.
It plunges into the current, leaping,
sliding, glistening. How gently
their shoulders slope over the bank,
their precarious balance undisturbed
by the dog. The poacher's tracks. Or our scent.

Wholly alert, they no longer tremble. They bow their heads
in praise of the present moment streaming with light
as if it were eternal, and it is, and they drink
for once without haste or fear.
Yes, this is the other world—
When we die we come here.

Among the Leaves

At dusk a lone nightbird drifts
and cries above the street. When
it quiets down we see how stars
begin to gleam among the leaves
of the tallest elms, far but clear.

As the dark deepens they shine
like the warning-lights on buoys
rocking beyond the harbor,
though we're happy to be walking here
on the bottom of the sea.

Meditation at Mill Creek

1
The wind arrives before the sharp-scented rain,
rustling the trees beside the creek. In full
flower dogwood tremble while they shed

their petals, pink and white, on the water.
Kneeling, you retrieve a blossom—veins
form a delicate fan which sustains its plush

bloom. We follow the petal-flecked current
where it eddies among rocks, tumbles,
splashes on. How long have we heard the geese

calling overhead? Walking out, we track
their clamor beyond the trees. Caught up
in the symmetry of their flight, its mystery:

How they maintain direction by suddenly shifting
formation—parting, reassembling—the flock
navigating by starlight, neurons, blood temperature.

2
Flying enormous distances with little rest,
what instinct instructs them, guides them—
black-tipped wings rising and dipping, rowing

north, white against the weighted clouds?
We'd like to see how their journey is repeated
in our lives—if it is—but the dusk deepens.

Not thunder, now. It's the rumble of a truck
or van descending from the mountain fire-
lookout as the storm breaks above the canyon.

3
Lightning cracks the low cloud cover—jagged
electric limbs flashing around us, plummeting
through the insulating air, missing the thistle

pines and dogwood; scorching the basalt gorge.
We've run into the steep draw only to stand
shivering. Hoping for a ride into town,

we watch the van approaching, its beams blurred
in the rain's glimmer, as the mind, too, branches out
brightly or darkly but always at hazard—

All community conjoined by what we think
is solitary: A dogwood's veins. The skein
of geese—their cries thrown across the sky—

Lightning that illuminates the blue Bookmobile
from the Rural Library Co-op, headlights groping
down the narrow road black and slick with rain.

Looking at the Man

1
Looking at the man who hangs on the tree
stripped bare, black

hair swirled with sweat
as if he had been running away

from his youth to climb
the spine of this hill

at noon while the heavens howl
then shut with a hush

to seal the sun in the tomb
of a winter night,

nine birds like leaves
that loop the hard hilltop
witness such weather.

2
Looking at the man and his mother

hunching herself the way women wait
in a downpour, watching

clouds cleave apart for the moment
no one doubts he's going to die

now that every song but pain is gone
from his eyes, his limbs

slack like a hawk nailed
by one brown wing to the barn door

finally falling limp, crying out
when the lust in his eyes grows dim

we are moved to believe
the blue skull
of the sky hears him.

Morning Song

As a river of mist rises from the valley
(but disappears in the quietly blue air)
fenceposts stand wet and dark.

The gate is slow to move in the sun.
Moist grass tall enough to hide
a threatened nest gleams at our feet.

After the shadow of a hawk
scissors its wings, once, twice,
then crosses unswerving over the field

that bright stillness is forgotten—
Meadowlarks sing as if each morning
we're seeing this world for the last time.

Doctor Paracelsus

1

Friend, I urge you: Search
your soul to discern
its sacred creatures—
Parents and children,
angels and demons.
Beasts or divine shades.
Even those who wear
a natural shape—
Here I speak of owls
and the furtive fox.
Toiling toads or sly
spiders—how they steal
our thoughts!—Song sparrows,
the lusting ram. Mare
and foal frolicking.
Insidious lice.
House cats that out-stare
the sun. Grackles grown
plump with esteem. Which
of such entities
answer to your own
imagination?

2

Trust these and you will
not be betrayed. Love
and you will not be
deceived. For the heart

is the doorway from
the dark dream. By this
I mean night or day
shines within us for
our galaxy dwells
deep in the belly—
a sea of stars and
each is eternal
illumination;
each one is ever-
lasting light! Which
is why I believe in
all men or women
when we awaken
we will find heaven
whole and unbroken.

Fishing the Sky

Once the heron sets
sail its shadow
harrows the tide-
pools, the shallows.
Soapy foam fills
each seep it waded.
Risen, the bird
outreaches the broken
beach (ripe bushes
no bill probes
for berries.)
>   Snaps
Shellfish aloft . . .
Lets them plummet,
splatter the rocks.

Diving, devours them.

Windward it wanders—
The sun is a net
to drag below its gaze. (Trolling,
it awaits the least
flash,
>   flicker
of scale
or fin
in a trough.)
>   Slowly
rows its wings,

fishing the sky
over the shadow-
crossed shore,
the glimmering sea.

Black Water

Black blazing night. My heart
pounding, I hear
your heartbeat under my hand,
we pause beneath the trees
to kiss. Hike on down
from the high woods.
                        Loud
rush of wings. Wind falling
silent in the pines. You and I
follow the old bear trail trampled
clear to the shore: Rocks,
rubble, sedge grass tall
in the shallows. No moon
on the lake. Stars
spark and shine.
                        Alone
through the dark we watch
two ducks tuck in, drift together.
On the pine shore we lie down—
I want to feel your breasts turn
firm in my palm. Your tongue
in my mouth when our legs open.
In the moist fur the fold
encloses me. And when we part
I want to lie with you
the way night lies on deep water—
On the slow breathing lake
two wild ducks float

side by side, asleep
on still water. Black water.

Now

1

When we lived in deep dusk the mind of man or woman
was a night-blooming flower. The bulbs
were buried in the black earth. Now we begin
to remember the story of everlasting night:
When we dream and desire no redemption.
The elemental pull of the moon
over the pearl-seeded sea
of our souls. Night of unknowing
that shelters the golden bees,
poppies, a slim green snake.
Awake in the fragrant dark we taste
its salt on our lips when we kiss.

2

Forgive us—in a brief and busy history
blood draped the chambers inside each skull,
the walls of the mind were crimson.
The blood we spilled every day flowed into the fabric
of our lives, the bright flag of our belief.
We invented Europe and original sin and absolution.
We invented witchcraft, heresy, and the balance of power.
We determined the mind of man
must rule the body of the earth
where we record the millisecond of each missile-launch.
We calculate a diminished response time.
We acknowledge our margin for error.

3
We remain uncertain of the morning
when the apple orchard flowers.
The sun of midsummer ripens and falls
and deer slip down from the high meadows.
Bells ring across the valley. Walking home
from school our children ask why do we die?
At dusk a steep snow quiets the foothills.
Earth glows in winter light.
The luster of a pearl—
the moon rising
in the night
sky.

V

Summer Night

Night of south winds—night of the large few stars!
Still nodding night—mad naked summer night.
Walt Whitman

Tree House

1

All morning with my wife I labored
over that house, then left it
for our children
to devise the door. Left them, too,
the rope ladder. Still its spiral rungs
like stigmata burn
the pattern of their purpose in our flesh.

Together on the porch we take our rest—
We climbed so long
in and out of that tree
my arch bears the ache of each branch
underfoot. Unable effortlessly
to open, my palm remembers the grip
of those limbs, the hammer, the rope.

2

Like trout our children float in the shadows
of forked boughs. In the bare-bones house
built of baling wire, weathered wood, leafy roof,
nothing more substantial than their dread
of falling hard to the earth forms
their floor. They hide their faces. Headfirst
they emerge, they spatter paint on the door!

They cry—first fright, then joy!
Leaves glow with glee,
feet and hands learn the boles

that bear weight. Up and down
the trunk and leaping
branches, laughter crawls
across the cool afternoon.

3
Shadows flood the grass and sink
the odd artifacts
of our hours: hammer, handsaw, paint-
brush stained blood
red. Ruler, pliers. Paper
plates, plastic cups. The bucket
of chicken bones plucked clean at supper.
Forgotten too when they sleep is the rope
coiled neat as a molecule within
night's body, every rung
imprinted in us now.
Overhead a tree whirls
across the sky. A tree of stars
where our children stir and dream

they are flying from limb to limb
among the shining creatures taking shape
the moment the mind makes them out—
The Hunter, two Bears, the Princess, the Swan,
dance on the dark floor of heaven.
Dance like the light that leaps in our eyes
when our children climb down from the tree at dawn.

The Storm Cellar

The tornado dragged the trees through the powerline
in a blast of sparks. Darkness. Lightning balls
blazed out in the kitchen sink. Mother in tears,
we carried candles down the cellar stairs—
Jars of plums from a pantry shelf spattered
the floor. "Watch for glass!" Father held her arm,
side-stepping skis, the ancient Zenith radio.

A wavering light searched the damp walls. It found
our sled. The oak crucifix. Over the musty sofa
a portrait of my uncle before the Navy
shipped him across the Pacific. I switched
the radio on. Line still down. My brother
wrestled me to the floor. "The candles!
Careful," Mother cried. "Dad, why don't we pray?"

Grandfather's baseball signed "Babe" and tan with age
climbed his arm, rolled behind his neck, vanished!
He fished a harmonica from his pants to play
his train medley: *Wabash Cannonball,*
Casey Jones, Rock Island Line, Railroad Bill.
We sang faintly. Until my father bowed
gravely, braced himself, rose onto his hands.

His breathing stertorous but his body still,
keys, comb, a penknife spilled from his pockets.
My brother followed, feet in the air. Counting
the candles, afraid I'd fall, I heard the storm
pound in my ears. Suddenly the radio,

sputtering static, delivered news of the war:
"Islands shelled . . . Strafing . . . Retreat denied . . ."

After the storm stomped across the prairie
only the downpour persisted. We toppled
to our feet. Stood gasping. And giddy with fright
forgot to pray though thunder shook the house.
God whose gaze is the lightning flash—red
and gold—that shreds the summer heat; whose voice
uproots the pine that snaps the powerline:

Remember the scorched sink. The drumming rain.
Mother sobbing in the plum-fragrant night.
God, in your mercy, remember we stood on our hands
while candles danced before our eyes like stars.
By flickering light we saw the world turning
upsidedown. It was warm and dark. In our
fondness and misfortune we were weeping and singing.

Raccoons

1
First the thick woods above the river.
Then nightfall as the road plunges
through wide farmland and the wind smells so fresh
I imagine cornflowers nodding in the fields.
No, it's the new-mown grass—
An electric fence flanks the artillery range
where the prairie is cropped short to discourage fires.
Tonight the barracks are too warm for blankets;
the troops twist in their sleep. Wind sweet as grass
bathes the tanks, somber in their stillness.
And huge howitzers. The half-dozen mortars in place
for morning maneuvers. I drive faster, unswerving.
Then, suddenly, slow. Just ahead they shine . . .

2
A low chain bobbing beside the road. I can't see
what joins them until they stop, struck blind
by my oncoming lights—
Seven in all return from their raid
of the garbage bins behind the mess hall.

Mother with your young
fed now, heading home,
to meet the danger in our eyes
you cover yours with that black mask.

You know death in our hands, in our speeding cars.
The dream in the turret of the starlit tank.

The sleep in the cool throat of the cannon
while the arc of the mortar shell grows more precise
than men or women, game birds, the stray cub crossing the road.

3
Mother of the low-bending, sure-footed night,
with your belly slung above the earth
you assert your body between the bones
of six plump cubs and the steel and chrome
rattling toward you. Driving on
under the green wind and the stars burning
above the fields, close-cut, prepared for war,
I pray to you
not for your life but for mine
as we pass—
Your brood behind you, bellies full,
trotting down the road through the black-eyed night.

Nighthawk

1
I love this storm—you do, too—its flash and glimmer!
Lost Child Creek rises, roiled by rain, the overflow
seeping under the red rocks in the meadow,
swelling the white roots of the weeds.

Lightning scars the dark sky behind the pines.
We run through the thicket—
rain sweeps the clearing.

"I can't go home. Hold me."
"Are you crying?"
"Hold me."

2
Who can sleep?
This gentle insistent
rain all night
saying your name.

3
The morning gleams with wet
light as we walk the meadow
where you discover blue
larkspur. Wild iris.

Encompassed by the marsh
marigolds, fawn lilies,

spindly stickweed, a rain-
pool ripples the sun.

It shakes itself, shining.

4
"I'm not like this. I'm not!"

5
After you leave
the leaning aspen
shimmer in the water.

6
White-tail deer browse for berries until twilight
draws them down to the lake. They disappear
into dusk. Above the trees a nighthawk
revolves around its solitary cry.

A tune too shrill for joy—
Peeent-peent. Peent-peeent.
What does it seek in the deep sky?

What does it hope to find
on the darkening earth?
The first stars burnish the lake
and silence falls like a black wind.

Songs without Words

> The emotional reach of music, the way it
> unleashes feelings . . . free of language . . . the
> wordless response to music . . . seems to stir deep
> portions of our psyche, what I want to call the
> body's mind.
> Elizabeth Dodd, *In the Mind's Eye*

1 *Water Music*

A barge with groaning timbers broke the stillness.

When the sun stroked your breasts
the orchestra of morning
flew over the toiling river.
The city of my blood knelt in its silent streets.

2 *Wine Festival*

The harvest has been blessed
yet there is no
music. Spirit
of root, vine, blood, bone,
why do you sing so low?

3 *Waking*

Wind off the water rustles a stand of aspen.
The pair of otters basking
on the blue mudbank dream what happens.

Summer thunder. Its boom and shudder.
We roll toward the middle of the bed,
embracing. Our tongues touch. Our eyes open.

4 *Blame*

Autumn—the first cold night.
As if it's our fault
three old peacocks sit
screeching in the trees.

5 *Those Two*

In the marketplace the proud Arabian
stallion glowers over
his timbered stall
at the modest mare
penned nextdoor.

6 *This, Too, at Dusk*

Men and women form a ring.
Voices intermingling
with the rising smoke.

Skewered on a spit
above hot red coals
a roasting goat.

7 *Memory*

The hour is late. Starlight pours
like rain through the storm-torn
roof of the covered bridge
over Lost Child Creek again.
Beneath the bridge the current
thrums, thrums in the dark.

8 *After the Storm*

Awake—it shivers
all night—this pool
of rainwater in
the grass beneath
the belly of the moon.

9 *Ancient Music*

Praise now the god who taught leaves all their songs.
Who made an ancient music walking in the weeds.
Who whistles soft when death has filled the lungs
of lovers with nesting birds; our eyes with restless seeds.

The Mare

Prepared to survey the mustangs and treat
on site any injured or diseased
we approach the fractious herd equipped
with cameras, notebooks, the raw scent
of our inquisitiveness. Our need.
Most days these, alone, cost us their trust.

They're wild, quick-witted, swift. Difficult
to secure and examine. Female
or male will keep a measured distance

grazing the mountain meadow, dawn
to sundown. (Nights are little better.
Their sleep like ours seldom soothed by dreams.

More often disturbed.) So, at midday,
the gaunt mare surprises us. The herd
has banished her. Outfought and outrun,

she's been driven off—pursued by young
ill-tempered rivals. Famished, mewling,
she hobbles into camp. A taut creature

crippled by fear. Her tail hangs clotted,
flies ravage her face. The sharp ribcage
is barred with scars. Still with modest grace

she tolerates two vets who guide her,
untouched, to the rear of my truck. She

wants water first. Never lifts her head.

With eyes half-closed she begins to eat
the fresh sweet hay. Her breathing is slow
and shallow. Her shoulders quiver
twice before she quiets and her being
has stepped into another world. Where
no one can follow. Not now. Not ever.

Summer Night

In the dark a loud spattering that streaks
our windows. A hush. A downpour. Water
probes slack gutters and uncertain shingles.
The rain is blind but it finds what it seeks.
Along the arching limbs of an elm it searches,
then plummets into meticulously weeded beds
where pools gather, bubbling in the black loam.

A torrent now that wakes all the flowers.
Big blowsy roses, glossy azaleas.
And the bold, fragrant, half-mad gardenia
that loves attention and never blushes.

The house grows cool; shivers. After the whine
of a car—at this hour—on the wet street,
I listen to your breathing beside me.
Darkness and rain. In our corner room late
at night we lie together and won't sleep
because the soul longs for darkness and rain.

Enjoy the Land

A sudden shower soaks the granite slope.
The sky clears, the moonlit grasses glisten,
already the runoff tumbles splashing
into Deer Creek. I'll cross it four or five
times walking downstream. Water cascading
over rocks, rushing beneath the aspen
and oak that shelter the foothills, spilling
from skeletal ancient flumes, then, slowly
chuffing through a network of flood channels,
greening the valley. Tireless as the blood
that sustains love and braves any distance.
Or why does a man seek the solitude
that troubles him? In the dripping shining
quiet I miss my son in Nebraska
and my two daughters in California.
Here a full moon illuminates the old
tribal burial ground. Long neglected,
it's overgrown. The thicket opens
where summer herds—mule deer and blacktails—
at dusk travel tenacious zigzag trails
into an upland meadow. Which they share
with coyotes, squirrels, jays, vultures. "Enjoy
the land," Thoreau wrote, "but own it not."

I haven't learned to let go. May never learn
to live without the hope that haunts parents,
the weight of our regret. I pick my way
through outcrop and thistles onto a path
worn by campers, hikers. Hearing the wind

riffle the wild pasture. A bull's skull
ringed by lupine holds its cupful of snow-
white rainwater, a lambent light, the moon
more at home in the meadow than I am—
Long after his children are grown a man
still carires his family in his heart.
Turning back, I follow the footpath down
through rippling grass. With luck I'll arrive
after dawn: the sun like a seed sprouting
from the hayfield and the almond orchard,
the roadside patch of vetch. Daylight blooming
beside the black road into town. Always
we long for those we've loved in the silence
of what was whispered, wept, or left unsaid.
Now because we bear them with us—welcome
companions—each of us is more than one
man or woman. A city of souls, we greet
the morning among the living and the dead.

George Keithley's epic poem *The Donner Party* was a
Book-of-the-Month Club selection and has been
adapted as a play and an opera. He and his wife live in
Chico, California. His recent collections include *The
Starry Messenger* (Pittsburgh).

Breinigsville, PA USA
21 March 2011
258013BV00003B/2/P